The Little
Wanted

An American Folktale Retold by Betty Erickson
Illustrations by Ryan Durney

Little Rabbit had soft white fur, long pink ears, shiny red eyes, and a puffy tail. But he didn't like the way he looked.

When Squirrel raced by,
Little Rabbit wished for
Squirrel's big bushy tail.

When he saw Porcupine's pointy quills, he wished he had quills. When Duck waddled by, he wished for her floppy orange feet too.

Little Rabbit kept on wishing.
But his mother said,
"I love you just the way you are."

One day Groundhog heard Little Rabbit wishing and said, "Go to the Wishing Pond and look at yourself in the water. Turn around three times and make a wish."

So Little Rabbit hopped
to the Wishing Pond.
He saw himself in the pond
and turned around three times.

He sat down to think of a wish.
While he was thinking,
a red bird came by for a drink.
Little Rabbit saw the bird and
wished for red wings.

Suddenly, he could feel wings beginning to grow.
The wings grew and grew.

Then Little Rabbit went off to show his mother his red wings. "Mother Rabbit! I'm home," he called. But, Mother Rabbit didn't know him as she had never seen a rabbit with red wings.

It was getting dark,
so Little Rabbit asked Porcupine
if he could spend the night with him.
But Porcupine didn't know him either.

Little Rabbit was tired and cold and hungry. He sat down on the path and cried. Groundhog found him and took him home for the night.

The next morning, Little Rabbit tried
out his wings, but they didn't work.
He got caught in a sticker bush
and Groundhog had to get him out.

"Don't you like your beautiful red wings?" Groundhog asked.

"No!" Little Rabbit cried. "No!"

"Then go back to the Wishing Pond and make a wish," Groundhog said.

So Little Rabbit hurried to the Wishing Pond.

He saw himself in the pond.
He turned around three times
and wished to be himself again.
Suddenly, the red wings disappeared.

Then he went home as fast
as he could hop.
His mother said, "My Little Rabbit,
you are home at last."
And he never went back
to the Wishing Pond again.